Johnny Indovina: My Bag of Secrets...The Words of Human Drama
Published by DIXSAMDEE Music
First Printing March, 1998

Executive Production: Lance Davis
Front Cover photo: Robert Butcher

Dedication:

This book is dedicated with thanks and love to all that have helped spread the word of

Human Drama.

My Bag of Secrets...

The Words of Human Drama

CONTENTS

Foreword:

So why a book...?

The first time I saw Human Drama play was at a small club called Madame Wong's West in Santa Monica, California. Some friends of mine had seen them play, became friendly with them, and they could not stop raving to me about what a great band they were. So I did it. I finally broke down and went with them. I can't imagine the difference in my life, had I not.

I'll never forget how amazed I was by the hugeness of the sound. I remember actually being surprised when, once the fog had lifted, and the lights were raised, I did not find an entire orchestra sitting there- for that was my first impression. The sound was so very big. I sat there quietly, and eventually I realized that I was being enveloped by the music, by Johnny's voice, by the words he sang. It was at that time that I knew why these five guys sounded like twenty. It was the honesty, the absolute real passion and intensity with which they played. Every note pierced my skin, every word pierced my heart, until finally I felt like Johnny had been looking straight into my soul. Needless to say, that was only the first of the many times I have seen Human Drama live.

To say that something as trite as a rock group can change your life might sound silly, perhaps even cliche. But if you are holding this book in your hands right now, and reading these words, then I am almost certain you know exactly of what I speak.

There is Johnny Indovina, the very nice guy who I have become lucky enough to call "friend." He's the guy that asked me to write this foreword for his book. And then, there is JOHNNY INDOVINA- performer. The man up on the stage, who I am still completely intimidated by, and am 100% in awe of. The guy who can still look straight through to my soul, and who somehow manages time and time again to write songs which do the same. It is because of him that I couldn't possibly refuse.

I think perhaps the reason Johnny the performer is so intimidating to people, including myself, is because when he sings we know that "he knows." There is no hiding from him, as he does not hide from us. I guess that is the difference between the two of him, and I imagine the two of all of us as well. When he is onstage, it is that innermost core of himself that he allows us to see, which brings out the innermost core of us, and forces us to actually feel our feelings, and acknowledge the emotion we so often disguise in our everyday life. I have always said that Human Drama was the best group catharsis I have ever witnessed. I have heard many fans say the same.

This book is an inside look into the words, thoughts, pictures, and genius that are Johnny Indovina; and the various manifestations that are Human Drama. It is for all of us that this book was made; the fans- a group in which I am eternally proud to include myself.

Enjoy-

Megan

ALL THE WORLD'S
A STAGE SET FOR

HUMAN DRAMA

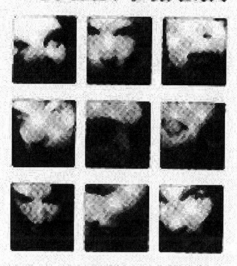

Their debut EP featuring
"OLD MAN"
"NOTHING I JUDGE"
"I BLEED FOR YOU"
"THE WAITING HOUR"

I Bleed For You

I can't tell a lie from an answered prayer
But I know
When I'm cut and burning

One day
I will put down the knife
Only when I trust
Another to hold it

I bleed for you
On my knees for you
I'll hand you heaven
Don't trade it for trinkets

This damn wind will change direction
It will stop you
Dead as you walk

Holding a nightmare
Called memory
That you led and
Held me to

I bleed for you
On my knees for you
I'll hand you heaven
Don't trade it for trinkets

"In a moment of panic after losing the woman I loved I wrote this. Maybe I should have shown more passion in the relationship instead of in hindsight. We are all guilty of this, aren't we?" ...Johnny Indovina

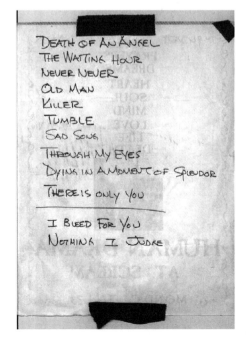

DEATH OF AN ANGEL
THE WAITING HOUR
NEVER NEVER
OLD MAN
KILLER
TUMBLE
SAD SONG
THROUGH MY EYES
DYING IN A MOMENT OF SPLENDOR
THERE IS ONLY YOU

I BLEED FOR YOU
NOTHING I JUDGE

Nothing I Judge

Here they come
Why do they scare me so
Like a child, what I don't understand scares me
The largest crowd I've seen
Whose chanting fills the streets
These hollow feelings make me eager to see

Take a look
You can never be anyone
You can never be anyone
If I say even if you are
You're making me run from Jesus
You're scaring me away, from Jesus

Nothing I picture nothing I judge
I tear down walls I don't trust as strong
My actions speak louder then your words
Patience builds a bridge, Insecurity starts war
Admit we can be wrong and we're as good
As we can be

Take a look
You can never be anyone
You can never be anyone
If I say even if you are
You're making me run from Jesus
You're scaring me away, from Jesus

Nothing I picture nothing I judge
I tear down walls I don't trust as strong
My actions speak louder than your words
You're making me run from Jesus
You're scaring me away
From Jesus
Don't scare me away

Nothing I Judge:

"I don't believe in any religion that is judgmental. In 1984 during Mardi Gras in New Orleans a preaching mob made their way through the streets harshly judging all who refused to join in the demonstration. A family trying to avoid the "in your face" preaching techniques moved to the other side of the street. The man was called a drunk, the woman was called a whore. This was done in front of their two small children. I watched from a window above. I thought about this incident and the effect it would have on the children. What if this was their introduction to the word god? How could they trust any god that would allow its followers to call the parents they love so much a drunk and a whore." ... Johnny Indovina

A word from the fans:

What Human Drama has meant, means, and always will mean to me... It seems only yesterday , when an outcast kid stumbled into the St. Bernard Civic auditorium to see what the latest Calamity had to offer... some group called "The Models."... Little did I know then how much Johnny's music would impact my life.

With school complete, career and relocations put me first in Houston, Tx then in Anaheim, Ca only to discover along the way that "The Models"... had become "Human Drama." ...I found myself homesick for New Orleans. This could sometimes be stated by Johnny's musical paintings of "White River", "Nothing I Judge", and "I Bleed For You" which seemed to somehow arouse feelings in me that were first experienced at home. But what was more evident was raw intensity in which Johnny led the band to pour out soliloquy.

...In any case I became a "Johnny Junkie." Johnny, thanks for making music, sharing your soul and painting musical tapestries that seemed to touch places in my heart that more often than not were left to my own private musings.

...What does Human Drama mean to me? Life is easy, living is hard, recognizing the passion of human experience is even more difficult, but capturing its essence in music to be replayed/experienced at will is a gift from god... that's what Human Drama is to me...

-Brian Anderson

Refugee from da' parish

Death Of An Angel

Death of an angel so beautiful to me
Shattered pieces fall to earth
Time can never heal

The story is over now, all points have been made
But when you hold out your hand
I don't see a thing

You can reach for the stars, but take what you get here
You can reach for the stars
But take what you get here

Was last December and all was milky white
Came December again and all is black
With hands to our mouths, we need food to live
But it's poison's nature to kill
If we choose to swallow

You can reach for the stars, but take what you get here
You can reach for the stars
But take what you get here

So far
So far, so far
So far, so deep
So deep, so deep
So deep it burns
I burn, I burn
Until I cry
I cry, I cry
I die, I die
I die, I die

"Sometimes it is not until after all the mess is made that we discover we
made it ourselves."...Johnny Indovina

I Could Be A Killer

Soft voice
Soft appetite
I'm hurt
But I'm alright

I'm still chasing echoes
But who is to blame
So call me a loser
But I could be a killer

Mythical tales
Are not what I write
Because these colored eyes
Don't want to fight

Now I might fall down
Succumb to your shove
And wondering, I know
That I could be a killer

I could be a killer

"A person's outward appearance does not gage the power he holds within. This lyric, as did the song, pointed me in the direction of what would become Human Drama. I wrote it in 1984, on my parents sofa. I think about it every time I'm at my parents' house in New Orleans."... JI

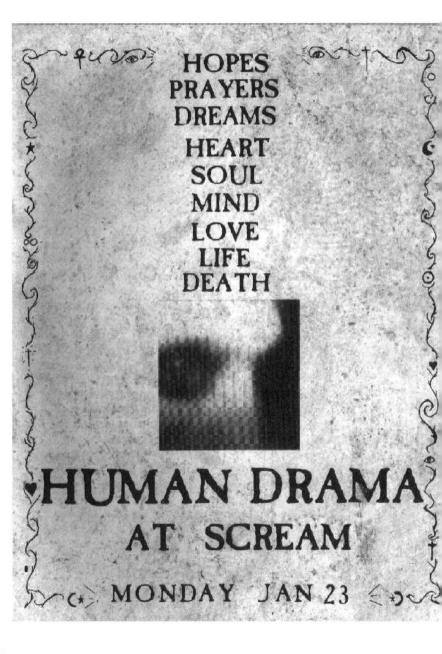

HOPES
PRAYERS
DREAMS
HEART
SOUL
MIND
LOVE
LIFE
DEATH

HUMAN DRAMA
AT SCREAM
MONDAY JAN 23

Never Never

Well behold I feel that breeze, coming back so strong
And the truth, I'm terrified. It's stronger then me still
I wish to the heavens, cross my heart
Pray god, give me strength
Support my will, renew the grace
May I remain, may I remain
A demon pulls monster will rise.Will I go down again?

Never never will I go
To the hell I used to know
Never never will I forget
The touch of the hand of love, happiness
happiness

I yell be gone! Demand again a heart confused by hands
The battle of good and evil is on, this time who will prevail
Cause I hear the sound of the rain
It's drowning out my heartbeat again
For every push with all my might a wicked push returns
Another time another place, but does it really change?

Never never will I go
To the hell I used to know
Never never will I forget
The touch of the hand of love
happiness

Temptation wraps a wicked cord, so tight I can't escape
I hear the sound of the rain. It's drowning out my heartbeat again
For every push with all my might a wicked hand pulls me down

Never never will I go to the hell I used to know
Never never will I forget the smile the joy the hand of love
Never never will I go to the hell I used to know
Never never will I forget the touch of the hand of love
...happiness

"A drug song."... JI

Tumble

Take your hands off of me. I've felt that touch before
Put to trance, a deep deep slumber
Held hypnotized
Get the hell out of here, my heart feels
But words I say come from someone else
Blind to what you are

Close as I come to catching my stumble
I tumble to you
Shields and armour bear no resistance
I tumble to you

I'm high as a kite. I've been this high before
I never dreamed such levitation could sink so low
Here I come crashing down. Here I lay like before
No images words or imagination to cushion my fall

Close as I come to catching my stumble
I tumble to you
Shields and armour bear no resistance
I tumble to you

To fly the wild blue yonder
Swimming crystal water
To open arms inviting they are
But you take it back, take it away

Do I get out alive?
What becomes of the scars
And why won't the hand that reaching to help me
Just leave me alone

Close as I come to catching my stumble
I tumble to you
Shields and armour bear no resistance
I tumble to you

Tumble to you

Through My Eyes

This is a happy new year's day. Here is where it begins
The sting of the cold I remember.
Only how little I noticed how bad it could hurt
I will see you on Easter. I see the rain stop
Confirmation, is it only a symbol? Made to be deadly in a little boy's eyes.
Soon it will be summer. Something would scream at me atop that hill
A few days was its existence
Forever there to be climbed in a little boy's eyes

I didn't fall. I jumped and I will jump again
Because I heard, I understood what was there to see.
If it hit me in the head, I'd duck the second time
I saw the world change through my eyes.

The wind blew hard. Came an eerie cool breeze
So brave, we heroes teased the storm
September what did we do to deserve you
An hour's destruction unjust, yet rectified

Brand new teen, it's the curse of Christmas
You can stack religion beside your childhood beliefs
Because soon you learn, you never will understand
Why your eyes see the joy through the tears

I didn't fall. I jumped and I will jump again
Because I heard I understood what was there to see
If it hit me in the head, I'd duck the second time
I saw the world change through my eyes

This is a happy new year's day
It took forever to get here but a moment to pass
All memory can't prepare for tomorrow
Through all of our years remain a little boy's eyes

I didn't fall. I jumped and I will jump again
Because I heard I understood what was there to see
If it hit me in the head, I'd duck the second time

I saw the world change through my eyes

Through My Eyes:

"A review of my life at age 13. At the age I started making a lot of my own decisions that would start me on the path of who I am today. My refusal to be confirmed in the Catholic religion is one subject touched upon." ...Jl

A word from the fans:

What Human Drama means to me:

Human Drama is music for all the emotions. It is sad when I'm down or uplifting when I'm up, and sometimes the other way around, but always it makes me feel connected to myself, my feelings — it doesn't tell me how I should feel but lets me draw my own conclusions about the song on an emotional level. It is simply music that everyone should have a chance to experience, especially live, because there is a power behind the tender sound, that I think cuts across all divisions, and that people from all walks of life can relate to.

-Kelly Kline

The Waiting Hour

When your bag of secrets opened up and spilled
That radiant glow just disappeared
You rained down from the clouds you were in

Sometimes we can be so blind
But how does pain so bad not bleed
You push, you push, sometimes you don't expect to fall
But it's the violent turning of the golden rule
A lifetime of hell for every minute of heaven

I know your heart is breaking
Here in the waiting hour
And I know it will never heal
Here in the waiting hour

So cross your fingers, or your heart
Your idle wish commands no more
The mirror you hate reveals all in this world you control
Just empty out that bag of tricks
Cause in this limbo they don't exist
Just like your vanity, your hopes, your prayers, your dreams
Now did you hear the thunder when you realized
Your very own hands reached in and tore your heart out

I know your heart is breaking
Here in the waiting hour
And I know it can never heal
Here in the waiting hour

I know your heart is breaking
I know your heart is breaking
And I know how it feels the first time
In the waiting hour

I know your heart is breaking
I know your heart is breaking
I know your heart is breaking

Just like mine did!

The Waiting Hour:

"One of three songs I have written that I consider perfect. The same woman that I neglected that brought forth "I Bleed For You" found herself in the same situation I was in. I had moved on. She called one day and said, "I don't know what to do. I just keep waiting and waiting. For you to call, or to come back, or this all to be a dream." I told her I knew of what she spoke. I had been there. So I wrote about it."... JI

A word from the fans:

Human Drama are a band that mean a great deal to me. I first heard them when I was at a very low point in my life and I felt that Johnny captured the emotions I was feeling, in a way I never could. This is especially true of the song 'The Waiting Hour'. The powerful emotion in Johnny's voice and the lyrics touched my heart the first time I heard the song. It is a song that will always remain dear to me.

Louise

Dying In a Moment of Splendor

I am a hero. I am an actor
I'm this violent shade of blue
I am newly discovered tension
Still confused by yesterday

I am a hero on a mission
Staking claims, yielding none
I am an artist with a vision
Seeing hell, his destiny

I know the simple sting of a tear
Sends the star crashing to earth

Dying in a moment of splendor
For a moment the glory and the death
Are one the same

I am an actor. So unfeeling
Then a flower, I am crushed
I am a villain, unstable and anguished
Then an angel, you trust

The heartless echo of memory
Sends the actor whirling twirling, falling to his knees

Dying in a moment of splendor
For a moment the glory and the death
Are one the same

I am a bubble, almost to bursting
Swollen by unrelinquishing pride
I am the shrinking remains of potential
Never growing as I should

Dying in a moment of splendor
For a moment the glory and the death
Are one the same

Heaven On Earth

Distance mocks my screams into the pale blue
That soon turns to gray, just before night
Just before the silver cuts through and I'm found spellbound
There's something for you, there's something for me
It's something to feel

I call this place heaven on earth. We can't create it
I call this place heaven on earth. I shake and shiver

Orange sky melt, melt into my heart
The bleeding sun drenches me again. It showers me again
Till I understand the simpleness of store bought dreams
When I look into your face, the sun or the rain
To you it is me

I call this place heaven on earth. We can't create it
I call this place heaven on earth. I shake and shiver
I call this place heaven on earth. We can't create it
I call this place heaven

And let us never grow if growing is forgetting
Where heaven is
Where heaven is

Twisting I turn
Turning I face
Facing I see
Where we will walk
And where we will live
Until heaven

I call this place heaven on earth
We can't create it
I call this place heaven on earth
I shake and shiver

"This is about my family. I was blessed, and I know it." ...JI

There Is Only You

In the loneliness of midnight
In the cool light of morning
Through the empty fields of midland

There is only you

When I am so weak I can't stand
When I move mountains
When I doubt all that I understand

There is only you

Close as I come to suicide
On the days I spend as king
There's no doubt, both are fantasy

There is only you

The evil art of deception
The endearing heart of one love
The escape that we are human

There is only you

God in me
He teaches me as I go
But the devil in me
He urges me to forget

And I forget

"This is about my mother, born Dixie Lea Bullock. I need only think of her and all troubles fade. I wrote it by the ocean, near Malibu, California."...JI

The World Inside I

I see a light shining in your eyes, reflecting a shimmering lie
A costumed clown disguised the same
Intrigued by the sun and the moon

Nothing ever changes. Nothing ever changes

Do you see the seasons change? Tell me if it has rained
When you look to the heavens do you see past the stars
Because they'll never answer your call

Nothing ever changes. Nothing ever changes

Do you remember the lessons that you learned
Do you realize what the years, the tears have meant
Love is your ocean. Filled with fear you jump in
You cling to the side of life, trying to escape

The enemy
You are the enemy
You are at war

On the outside I am strong. No pain no weakness will you find
Push aside confusion. I battle endlessly
A victor in a war of one. I see myself, I disappear

Don't try to save me
Don't try to save me
For I come here of my own will
Here I will stay

On the inside children play, trying not to remember that they have grown
Eyes staring at me. Move with me motion for motion
Until I turn, I spin in circles, reaching I am for the door

Don't try to save me
Don't try to save me
For I built this house with my hands

Here I will stay

The World Inside II

Reach out your hand grab the penny
A surface war yields shallow rewards
Clench your fist make your demands
But you are conquering the wrong enemy

Alone you lie naked and bare
Conscience a mirror
You steal from your soul to feed your ego
Outside you're a hero

But alone you lie
In the world inside
Alone you lie
In the world inside

God of material villain of spirit
The fortress you build you must live in
Betrayal of trust faith and allegiance
You fool everyone but yourself

Alone you lie naked and bare
Conscience a mirror
You steal from your soul to feed your ego
Outside you're a hero

But alone you lie
In the world inside
Alone you lie
In the world inside

"An in-depth look at superficiality. Those of you who consider yourselves friends of mine now or ever beware, you may be in this song. If it is any comfort I make a few appearances myself. Shades of this song would later appear in "Sad I Cry" from the album "Songs of Betrayal.""...JI

My Skin

I see forest, stars in the sky at night
I am dreaming, I dream as a child
When I was allowed
When all was simple
When nothing could penetrate my skin

I see youth
When frowns were stranger then smiles
Unworn faces full of life, not worry
I long to return, I want to still wonder
I want nothing to penetrate my skin

We were younger then
Each day that came, more we would grow
But we are older now
And each day that comes takes more of my life away

Unscramble
This whirlwind of thought in my head
Competition forced into
Deceit that trusting allows
Rid me this struggle
Let me grow, in a world of childhood innocence
Where nothing can penetrate my skin

We were younger then
Each day that came, the more we would grow
But we are older now
And each day that comes takes more of my life away

I can't explain all the love I've had in my life
And how sometimes I couldn't feel it
For picturing it gone
Love rescue me now
Hold me tight so that I never forget
And nothing can penetrate my skin

'So self explanatory it is painful..." ...JI

Tears

See the pictures on the wall, the glory of the faces
Who never understood at all, the power of the moment
Or where the moment could lead
When the power starts to fade, weak, we start to tremble
It becomes an avalanche
We are overtaken by a feeling burning to get out

Our tears
There is nothing we can do to dry them
Our tears
There is nothing we can do to dry them

A starry sky tonight could turn to storm tomorrow
If it does we must be brave, we must live through it
Fear only kills if we allow
But the power of my love reaches farther then my touch
And it is more real than any trick your mind can play
And any trick I've been the victim of

Our tears
There is nothing we can do to dry them
Our tears
There is nothing we can do to dry them

If only I could carry you away
If we really were all we need
We'd have to create another place that no one else has ever been
If only I could learn how to love as strong as the pain I feel
I could dry our tears

There is writing on the wall. I know because I wrote it
Says "It's ok to dream, and it's alright to promise.
Just don't promise what you dream"

Our tears
There is nothing we can do to dry them

Tears:

"Insecurities sometimes overtake love. The fear of being forgotten, that something has changed because of a physical distance from the person you love. I wrote this at Rockfield Studio in South Wales while recording the "Hopes Prayers Dreams..." EP. I was trying to heal myself.".…JI

A word from the fans:

Human Drama has always held a certain depth for me that few other bands and musicians have ever equaled. Johnny has blended the speech of the heart and the head, and the words that come despite both of them.
The music is a testimony to the darkness within us all, the lightness without, and the grey residue left over (afterwards). It is quiet desperation. It is raging empathy. It is an aural bloodletting.The ultimate catharsis. It represents that link which, I believe, binds us all together even when we feel utterly alone: emotion. Johnny brings all these things to the surface, almost making them tangible. And perhaps most important of all is that Human Drama has brought this honesty into a musical environment that can often appear stale and trite. They have carved a niche with the Greats... whoever those "Greats" may be for whoever is listening. I can only thank Johnny and Human Drama for the lyrics that bespeak of truth (ironic, sarcastic, painful, and paradoxical as it may sometimes be), and for the music that is just as poignant- from the simplicity of acoustic guitar and flute to the rich, complementary layers of percussion, strings, bass, guitar, keyboards. Thank you for bending the rules until they break.

-Beth Boettcher

"Caresses felt with upturned fingertips; the reverberations of your melting sostenuto"

Look Into a Stranger's Eyes

There you are. Standing on a stack of your thoughts
Alone once more staring at a lifeless body
Wondering aloud, "Am I so blind, not to see it coming?"
Answered inside by the simple dropping of your head

Look into a stranger's eyes
Fall into his trap
Curious and intrigued
Led down his wicked path of deception

Living a lie the hole keeps getting deeper
See the shapeless form where a man once threatened to grow
See the shell of love where eternity
Surely could have blossomed
In a pile of past lessons, never to be learned

Look into a strangers eyes
Fall into his trap
Curious and intrigued
Led down his wicked path of deception

Temptation's claws make a powerful man weak
A coward reasons
Name another who would be so strong
You mistake a tomb for a castle
The dead weight of sand for gold
And a smile for a moment
A fleeting moment can erase your greatest fear

Look into a strangers eyes
Fall into his trap
Curious and intrigued
Led down his wicked path of deception

Look into a strangers eyes
Fall into his trap
Curious and intrigued
Led down his wicked path of deception

Look Into A Strangers Eyes:

"I looked at myself in a mirror one night and honestly did not know the person I was looking at. I was exactly the opposite of what I proclaimed and wanted to be. Actually the key track on "The World Inside" album as far as concept. It best sums everything up. Or maybe just points out the root of our problems as imperfect beings."...JI

A word from the fans:

Sometimes Johnny...

Perhaps these things don't just happen, but somehow are promised quietly. You see there was Johnny, and he created music, not like some god, but like a mortal full of feeling. Eventually it had to be stumbled upon, even if it took years. I remember finding the promo for "Fascination and Fear" in some long ago record shop while on holiday in California. I had heard the name "Human Drama" and figured that it was worth a listen. For a year perhaps, the cd sat on a shelf next until I needed it. Life is, as I am sure you know, a strange little beast. Sometimes we hear someone saying what we feel we need to say.

Johnny said a lot that night and many to follow. You either love or hate him, the music. Either way you can't deny the passion, and perhaps the truth. Seeing Johnny live... was dramatic and thrilling... I am thankful for the journey, it is one I would not willingly take on my own.

-ryan michael painter

This Tangled Web

For caring is a breeze that blows by
And returns only when, only when it wants to
So cry, cry little angel forever because

You can't wrap your arms around the wind
Within lie the reasons for
This tangled web we weave

For love at once my shield and terror
Destination and cause for living today
And wanting to die tomorrow
Why, why is my whole life spent chasing my demise

You can't wrap your arms around the wind
Within lie the reasons for
This tangled web we weave

In my face you see the torture lines from days gone by
But I was never touched these scars have risen from within me.

For memory take a knife it's quicker
Plunge it deep into my soul
Go ahead make me a weaker man
And cry, cry little angel forever because

You can't wrap your arms around the wind
Within lie the reasons for
This tangled web we weave
This tangled web we weave
This tangled web

"The second of the perfect songs. Usually I remember where I was when I wrote a song. I remember nothing about the writing of this. But I remember how I felt. Sometimes you just will not let go of someone you love even though you know you should. I love this song."...JI

Fascination and Fear

In stillness so much motion inside
In silence within I hold a deafening cry
My needs can never be satisfied
For my love will never be realized

I can almost feel your heart beating
See confusion in eyes so clear
The line between fascination
And fear

I battle a thought every second
For I don't feel as I was taught
I want to swim the river forbidden
I want to climb the mountain denied

I can almost feel your heart beating
See confusion in eyes so clear
The line between fascination
And fear

My needs can never be satisfied
For my love will never be realized

I can almost feel your heart beating
See confusion in eyes so clear
The line between fascination
And fear

"I was in a club one night leaning against the wall, (my normal position), and I saw a young boy who seemed to be about 18 standing close to the dance floor. The club leaned heavy toward a gay, lesbian and bondage crowd. He seemed to want to join the masses that were dancing, but was hesitant. I suppose he was having a battle between what he actually felt, and what he was taught."...JI

Winter's Life

The leaves have gone brown, fallen to the ground
The mist that wets my face will surely freeze by sundown
As sure as winter comes, it drags with it its sadness
Another year gone by. One less left to live

I have often spent Christmas searching for reasons
That I never found. I never dreamed I would

But all has changed
I feel a new heartbeat
In your eyes
I'll always see winter's life

You are the warmth I feel through the coldest December
The single ray of sun that shines on a cloudy day
You are the proof that heaven answers
The fire to warm my freezing hands
And the color on the grayest of days

All has changed
I feel a new heartbeat
In your eyes
I'll always see winter's life

Love rain down on me. Erase the weight of the world
Climb upon my shoulder. You are the weight of my world

I'll suffer the wind . And with each shiver remember
Winter is not the end, only a reminder
That a brilliant day is on the horizon
And as each year goes by so builds my treasure of love

All has changed
I feel a new heartbeat
In your eyes
I'll always see winter's life
In your eyes I'll always see winter's life

Winter's Life:

"I became friends with Ian Broudie, now of the Lightning Seeds, when he was brought in to produce my first two releases on RCA. He called to tell me he and his wife had just had a baby boy. I felt the joy in his voice. Riley Broudie was born in winter time. I imagined that no matter how cold and dreary winters continued to be through the years in Liverpool, England, the remembrance of the child's birth while watching him grow would always make for a glorious time. It's a happy song. One and counting..." JI

A word from the fans:

I saw the band perform at Nemesis in Ft. Lauderdale about a year ago now. It had to be the most powerful show I have ever seen.... It's a pity that I wasn't familiar with more of the songs played. I happened to catch the warm up before doors opened when "I Could be a Killer" was played. It was at that moment that I knew that the show was going to be amazing. I had a chance to talk to Johnny before and after the show along with the rest of the band... I asked him what his favourite album was and he told me "The World Inside". I hadn't heard it at that point but stumbled on it a few months afterwards. It is INCREDIBLE to say the least. There are very few bands that can exhibit such emotion in their work. It's something that I can appreciate each time I listen to the album (and other releases). I felt kinda silly asking for autographs from everyone, but I don't regret it now. It was an undescribable pleasure meeting Johnny and I just want him to know that he is a profound inspiration on my own musical work. I hope to hear much more from him and the others in the future. If there is a tour in the future, Human Drama is more than welcome in South Florida again. .... hopefully when and if it does come about, HD could maybe grace the stage for open ears and open hearts.
Keep up the great work, and never EVER take the emotion out of the art of song weaving that is done so well........ :)

Sincerely,

Acheron

A Million Years

Push a pin into my arm. I will bleed like anyone
Pull it out and I forget
On a trail blazed with words. One that I was lost upon
The road that I depended on, I follow no more
Tortured man take your hand, take it from the fire now
Place it in cool water

A hypocrite is one who prays only when he feels pain
It's time to open your eyes. So open your eyes

I could wait a million years
Look into a billion eyes
To find another love like this
I could wait a million years

The slamming door the unseen wall
The hurt I never could forget, I struggle to remember
And take my hand from the fire refusing all intended scars
You are cool water. Into you, I swim

I could wait a million years
Look into a billion eyes
To find another love like this
I could wait a million years

Held still in one place for too long
Gone blind to the miracle of saving
I pray this angel in my eyes was put here to save my life
Through your eyes I feel your soul
What I feel I must believe. What I believe I live
And this coming from a man who clenched
The truth so tight in his hands. Then opened to find evil
Found trusting love again

I could wait a million years, look into a billion eyes
To find another love like this
I could wait a million years

A Million Years:

"Written for the person that ended my 'Waiting Hour'."... Jl

A word from the fans:

Being a fan, the music to me means everything. The past albums to the recent ones are like stairs. Growing with me as I age and every time I re-listen to certain albums they bring me back to that point in my life where I am happy or sad. Like the pages of my life.

-Cindy Woon

Color Me Red

I often drift away far into another day
I answer questions complete the rhyme
Relive the beauty of another time

It's the calm before the storm

Color me red because I'm on fire
Direct me to a raging sun
Color me red because
I'm on fire

Time can't heal every wound
What seems faded returns soon
Memory strikes in its wicked way
Hatred devours the pleasure of a new day

It's the calm before the storm

Color me red because I'm on fire
Direct me to a raging sun
Color me red because
I'm on fire

The fire burns from what remains
Of all my ignored fear
And I'll burn until only ashes remain
I welcome the first wind to come

Color me red because I'm on fire
Direct me to a raging sun
Color me red because
I'm on fire

I'm on fire
I'm on fire
I'm on fire
...only ashes remain

The Sound of the Rain

Is that starlight shining in your eyes
Or is your heart on fire again
I have felt the flames until immune I've become
Disillusioned by love
Inescapable fate

I know it's coming
I'll be waiting
I hear the sound of the rain

An angels face
Fragile emotions fights monsters
Made from fairy tale tales
So delicate tender with strength unexplored
Well this dragon's been slayed again and again

I know it's coming
I'll be waiting
I hear the sound of the rain
The sound of the rain

So through every season
The devil grows stronger
Until smolder he does
When the rain comes again
Until smolder he does
When the rain comes again

I know it's coming
I'll be waiting
I hear the sound of the rain
The sound of the rain
The sound of the rain

Father Sing

I am a child, but I am growing, changing
Training my thoughts to be
I am the seed encouraged to dream
And nourished with food from your heart

I want your love. I want to know who you hate and why
I want everything good and bad. All of you, inside me

Father sing
The song that still makes me cry from years ago
When you sang to a little girl
You sing to me still
With a voice so loud and strong
Father though you are gone
You remain with me

You protect me, you make me aware
That the love inside these walls won't always exist outside
My symbol of strength all powerful in my life disappeared
And I cried

But I remember the first music I ever knew
I hear your voice. I feel you here

Father sing
The song that still makes me cry from years ago
When you sang to a little girl
You sing to me still
With a voice so loud and strong
Father though you are gone

You remain with me

"A friend of mine told me a beautiful story about her father who died
when she was very young. Her only memory was that of him playing his
guitar. The guitar stayed around the house long after he was gone. It
was a very moving story. I played it to her and she said she loved it."...JI

Voices

Innocent, afraid
Thoughts create an adult play
Too scared to cry
Walk on by
Penetrating eyes seem to see all, witness a lie
Resist command
Walk on by

I will never take my life

Mother's only son
Behind a mask a world unknown
That speaks to him
Walk on by
I am so sad says the voice inside his head
In a familiar voice
Walk on by

I will never take my life

Accept no blame if I give in
The boundaries of my mind
Reach farther then you see

Sometimes it's so loud
It is so clear what I hear
Is what I feel
Walk on by

What defines strength, accepting life
Or choosing to die
What do the strong decide
I walk on by

I will never take my life

Fading Away

I can't tell what is right, what is wrong
What is far, what is near
Can't distinguish between truth, and lies I fear

I am fading
I am fading
I am fading
Fading away

I can't find my strength
I really don't cherish the search anymore
I'm left without breath
From making points I won't make anymore

I am fading
I am fading
I am fading
Fading away

I feel no need to borrow the crutches I borrowed before
Or to make another speech whose theme
Justifies what I am

I am fading
I am fading
I am fading
Fading away

I can't take the guilt
I feel like a thief when compared to my father
He fed me then, he feeds me still
What have I ever done

I am fading
I am fading
I am fading

Fading away

Fading Away:

"A song to honor the hard work my father had to do to provide a home and a happy childhood for me. Sometimes I don't think much of what I am. I feel I have taken a long vacation compared to what my father did. He made many sacrifices that I have never had to make. I have so much respect for him."...JI

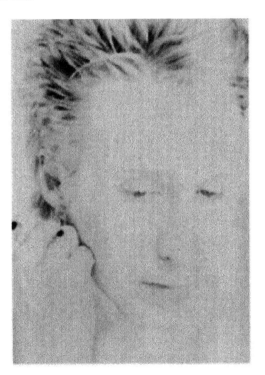

A word from the fans:

Human Drama isn't something you can just listen to...their music reaches inside of you and pulls something out.

darla...

Another Fifty Miles

Put one foot before the other
Brother, there is no turning back
You have turned around before
To find all you had built destroyed

Take your hammer and your nail
And all the love shared without condition
In your hands it must remain
And not until the grounds of truth do you lay your stake

Tomorrow you will walk another fifty miles
At night fall you will rest your weary head
If when you wake you find the rain
Has found you once again
Today walk another fifty miles

Blow cold wind rise high tide
Darkness show your howling sound
Mountain steep, I face you now
No longer will I seek the hidden path

Tomorrow you will walk another fifty miles
At night fall you will rest your weary head
If when you wake you find the rain
Has found you once again
Today walk another fifty miles

At everything that I called home
At every fledging empty soul
That stole the name I call my own
I won't cast another stone
I will walk on

"The first song I wrote after moving to New York in 1992. I take the blame for standing still at many points in my life. Reveling in pain, and accepting it. We are all responsible for our choices. This song is that acknowledgement and my solution."...JI

This Forgotten Love (1992)

See the water running through my hands
Fight to cleanse the stain again
Feel the chilling wind rush by it tries to push all from memory

Pick up the pieces of discarded trust
I must learn to form that word again
Remove the blind from blackened eyes
That were told they did not see

Shield the sunlight from my eyes
It's been so long since I have seen who I am
I used to feel so much. Search please let us touch
This forgotten love

Hear the echo of wasted words ricochet in my emptiness
As the raging flame of passion scorned reflects on my frozen skin

Shield
The sunlight from my eyes

I couldn't see in my submission. The chains were attached to nothing
The word love cannot love for you
The word love, it cannot love for you
Beneath the shell in darkness waits a timid heart
To beat again for another
And these blackened eyes and bloodstained hands
Wait to give and receive

Shield
The sunlight from my eyes
It's been so long since I have seen who I am
I used to feel so much. Search please let us touch
This forgotten love
What has this beating done
What has love become
Search and we will find
This forgotten love

This Forgotten Love:

"Along with "The Waiting Hour" and "This Tangled Web". a song I consider to be perfect. The most beautiful thing I have ever written. I wrote it over a seven hour period in February of 1992 and performed it for the first time at the "World Inside" record release party. I found true love. And it was."...Jl

Forever

Lay me down under clouds of silk
To within an inch of love you torture
Without words all is said
In your eyes the future told

What I feel
You must give
Forever
Forever
What I give
You must hold
Forever
Forever

Press your lips to my heart. Release the breath of life into me
Tear the flesh that surrounds my fear
With the same hand heal the wound

What I feel
You must give
Forever
Forever
What I give
You must hold
Forever
Forever

You touch me and suddenly I have no past
My secrets I release willingly
Man and child together as one
Holding in my hands both knowledge and innocence

Lay me down
Under clouds of silk
To within an inch of love
You torture

It Is Fear

The light in my eyes
That shines through the night
It is fear
Fear
Intense as my will to live
Burning like a fire
It is fear
Fear

I feel I belong here
I feel it in my bones

Something our mortal hands
Just can't control
Is fear
Fear
Stronger then the will of man
Is the will of God
We fear
Fear

I feel I belong here
I feel it in my bones
If today is my last day
Tomorrow I fear no more

Where Our Weakness Lies

I carved my initials into your heart
Against your will
I handed the knife to you, I lie here still
Believe not what you see or hear
Only what you feel
I've seen the greatest love stories
Inception to climax to end

Our foolish pride
We must conquer all
In our mightiest words
Our weakness lies

Grand is your love for me
Naked there you are
Still I dare you go further
You lie there still
You see nothing I want stands before me
All I need lies beyond
So open the door from inside
Show me all

Our foolish pride
We must conquer all
In our mightiest words
Our weakness lies

Let The Darkness In

I feel a story coming on
A chance to raise a few questions
About the simple solutions that were the answers before

I see a tear running down
A silent plea I must put to words
You will interpret your own way
As I must live in its pain

This song is hurting like a thousand before
Maybe I should stop
Before I open that door again
And let the darkness in

But it's pounding so hard
I hold my head to drown it out
Then take my pen and write it down
Another of life's little miseries

That I try and understand
But I am swallowed up too fast
And down the road I'd like to walk
I tumble out of control

I feel an ending coming on
The final fact to your fiction
A heart and soul lay sinking
And all you want to do is sing along

Sing it loud until the last note ends
The bottle in my hand is reflecting again
You can disappear but I must stay
I feel another story coming on

I let the darkness in
Must let the darkness in
Let the darkness in

Let The Darkness In:

"This is about the original guitarist / songwriter for the band the Gin Blossoms. Shortly after he passed away a friend of mine who knew them told me about his situation with being removed from the band and his addiction to alcohol. I was moved to write this song."

As Love Comes Tumbling

Here
Where my innocence was left
In the wake of fear
In recollection I resign
Into the bluest sky I wonder
But into the blackest night it turns

As love comes tumbling down

I stand
Pen in hand a war of words
One verse points to all I want
Another points to all I know
Far from the pen lies the answer
But onto the paper pours my heart

As love comes tumbling down

The world inside is shaking
As I search for the line that will one day heal
But hold me now
Hold me now
Hold me now

Into the bluest sky I wonder
But into the blackest night it turns

All That Cuts Today

The pounding of the day wrecks passion and innocence
I can hardly hold back tears as it slips away
Passion and innocence slip away

I shake where I stand as it is taken from my hand
I said yesterday "there is no tomorrow"
There is no tomorrow but here I stand

And the world turns round and round
Morning opens my eyes again
Passing time will dull all that cuts today

Tired eyes begs for sleep
Today's story waits for the moral
Fuel for the fire. Never fading

But does it ever rest?
Yes sleep does come because time's the water
Time is the water that will douse the flame

And the world turns round and round
Morning opens my eyes again
Passing time will dull all that cuts today

I've taken all I've seen. Wrapped it up so carefully
With just my eyes I can't decide. I reach to truth but found a lie
So I keep it inside

And the world turns round and round
Morning opens my eyes again
Passing time will dull all that cuts today

And the world turns round and round
Morning opens my eyes again
Passing time will dull all that cuts today

Passing time will dull all that cuts today

Mr Storyteller

Tell me again if you will
Of this love that never dies
Explain to me again my friend
Where all I have given lies

Look me in the eye
As you reassure
The path you direct me to
Leads to love and truth

Once Mr Storyteller
This tale you tell was mine
But for arms warm and loving
Was a stranglehold of lies

"I was tired of hearing and giving speeches with the themes "it will work out" and "you will find true love.""...JI

I Wonder Why

The question
Is clear
My dear
Please answer

All of your lies
I wonder why

Blue

I see confusion in your eyes
A heartless shell exposed
Fragile are all lies.

I hear a need in your voice
Twisting turning thoughts that tie me up in knots

I feel a distance in your touch
Do you fear what you may feel?
The years they do insist

And hesitation in your wish
To find what has been lost, I know you will not look

The blue has fallen from the sky
And it has cast its hue
Over my heart
The blue that once did cover the sky
Controls my every thought
Exposing every lie

Crossing boundaries set in stone
Do we find friend or foe?
A tale that time will tell.

I cry you see no tear
I scream you do not hear
This cut will never heal

The blue has fallen from the sky
And it has cast its hue
Over my heart
The blue that once did cover the sky
Controls my every thought
Exposing every lie

"The sequel to the song 'This Tangled Web'."...JI

Tired

How many times will you extinguish
love's flame?
How many times will you deny
holding the water?
The coward has been played
The weakest plan ever laid
And I feel nothing
But tired

Why will you not
confront your tears?
How many more will you blame
For what they destroy?
The answer is clear
But you, you refuse to hear
And I feel nothing
But tired

The answer is clear
But you, you refuse to hear
And I feel nothing
But tired

Yeah I feel nothing but tired

I
Feel nothing
But tired

Yeah

"The point in a relationship when you stop addressing the excuses and start dealing with the reality of what is actually happening."...JI

The Silent Dance

A sign reading heaven
Lies in the ruin
Beside passion and sharing
And pieces of my heart

A stuttering heart beat
Finally surrenders
But with its last shallow breath
Reasons the struggle

The silent dance
Of the ghosts we left
Will forever end in each others' arms
We can remove what we see
What we feel will never leave
These four walls

A penny for my thoughts
Well the world for an answer
Did you think just by closing the door
We could be still what lives here

The silent dance
Of the ghosts we left
Will forever end in each others' arms
We can remove what we see
What we feel will never leave
These four walls

The Silent Dance:

"As I walked out of the apartment where the relationship had taken place for part of the four years it lasted, I took one look back across the room. I thought about all of the great things that had happened, all the fun we had. I saw myself sitting on the sofa with my guitar. I saw her sitting on the floor painting the furniture and mirrors and clocks that she painted so beautifully. I remembered how she would get up and kind of dance across the room to get whatever it was she needed. I remembered how it used to make me smile. I remembered the smile on her face. The relationship was over but what had happened there would never go away. Somewhere, somehow the dance goes on."...JI

Remember Well

This is for everyone
That I have ever loved
Remember well
I will never love again

This is to everything
That I have ever touched
Remember well
I will never touch again

All that I held dear
All has disappeared

To the hope I carried
Every second of everyday
I release you
I hope no more

To whoever it was
That I prayed everyday
Wherever you are
I ask no more

All that I held dear
All has disappeared

This is for everyone
That I have ever loved
Remember well
I will never love again

"That second when you simply give up and damn everything to hell. It usually only lasts a second."...Jl

HUMAN DRAMA

The 2nd Coming

★ 850 S. MAIN, ORL ★
FL 373-8345

Sat. March 3rd

Sad I Cry

Are these the roses of which you speak
Where you stop everyday to scheme
Of what color you will paint tomorrow
On the canvas hung today
For I am a dreamer
Who fears never living his dream
And what I wouldn't give
For just one embrace
I picture it now
And melt away

Sad I cry

Is that the sunset that moved you to tears
The colors they strike you so deep
It has risen on me every day of my life
But could never set without you
You are on a ship that is sailing
As I yell from the dock, "Come back"
For without the nerve
To chance the storm
We can never sail into the sun

Sad I cry

I am sad for my love for the painting
I can hang but never create
How the most vivid red orange sunset
Can only be color to me
I cry for my arms surround nothing
We only hold what we are
The dreamer will dream
The ship it will sail without him into
The sunset again

Sad I cry

Sad I Cry:

"I wrote this during the filming of the "My Skin" video. I had met someone who so openly was moved by the beauty of the simple things in life. I realized I had allowed my chaotic lifestyle to prevent me from even noticing these things. To this day I am sure to pay attention."...JI

A word from the fans:

When I think of Human Drama, I think of true emotion. The first time I heard Human Drama, I thought God another over-dramatic band, but than I sat and read the lyrics to "Nothing I Judge", and "the Waiting Hour". When I listened to them again it was clear this would be a band I'd love for life. Before the first song ended on The World Inside, I knew it'd be one of my top five albums. The depth of feeling in the lyrics, combined with moving music. It doesnt matter if I interpret a song differently from what Johnny had in mind when he wrote it, only the fact that it moves me, that I can relate to the experience, that it can express something I feel, so much better than I can myself. I can only say I'm glad that I didn't dismiss them after one listen.

-Brian Holt

The Puzzle

I found you there
In silence read
As time stood still
Twenty five years have passed

In patterned lace
You lie before me like life itself
A promise echoed by the tear that stays
Fast forever to my heart

The puzzle is complete today
She cast her book of dreams away

An angel flies, all is clear to her now
Though dark to my eyes
I trade forgiveness for the promise kept
Held forever in her arms

Every step I take, every sound I hear
Each day I wake
My world is ours, I feel your touch
Your world is mine

The puzzle is complete today
You've cast your book of dreams away

I fought until the chains that bound you
They broke my will
I will swim to you
Far across a river of tears

The puzzle is complete

"I knew someone once that just couldn't handle life and the hardships it brings. I remember thinking, "maybe she's right, maybe she doesn't belong here." She had started to convince me of this. I wrote this song pretending that she was gone. I really like this one."...JI

Emptiness

I am a slave
To all that I don't own
An afterthought
To who has cast me away
Who cares not how I feel
And how it haunts me
Or how little I sleep

I damn the miracle of sight
For what I have never seen
I have yet to feel love
All you ever taught me
Was the reality of pain

I have stepped into a thousand journeys
I have died a thousand times
But to my horror I awake
For it is not death
But emptiness I face

"About a woman who was given up at birth for adoption. The ultimate form of betrayal."....JI

Wave of Darkness

Oh! This wave of darkness
Home to only shadows
Part of our love has died
We drive for miles
But we have no destination
We have no destination

Wells form in baby blue eyes
Darting, asking questions
Stretching her arms out far
To be held
This child, she will never be held again
She will never be held again

She looks for answers still
As recent as yesterday
But nothing comes
Only visions of highway 99
The brightness of the crossing line
Reflects father's eyes on highway 99
On highway 99

Oh! This wave of darkness, when will it be shed
'Till the day every step she takes
Be it left or right
Still leads her into the fire
Still reaching out
Crying baby tears
For a mother's arms
That let her go on

Highway 99
The brightness of the crossing line
Reflects father's eyes
On highway 99
On highway 99

We Walk Alone

Frozen as I feel, I live moment to moment
Fast smiles do disappear, changing moment to moment
But nothing will come or go without our pulling and pushing
The pictures we paint, they bring out our tears

We walk alone
Into the treacherous water
Alone into the dead of night
We walk alone into the hands of strangers
And into the love that keeps us walking on

Heard of a tangled web, If only I had seen it
Was touched by the kiss of death
I didn't feel any different after
Pull away from that web. It stretches but never gives way
The poems we write, they bring out our tears

We walk alone
Into the treacherous water
Alone into the dead of night
We walk alone into the hands of strangers
And into the love that keeps us walking on

Too many strangers' eyes have laid upon my soul
Too many, too many sure hands have let me go

To walk alone
Into the treacherous water
Alone into the dead of night
We walk alone into the hands of strangers
And into the love that keeps us walking on

HUMAN DRAMA
SPECIAL BENEFIT SHOW
TO HELP FRIENDS IN NEW ORLEANS
ALSO HELPING OUT:
members of Kill for Thrills
FRANCIS X
CAFÉ FLESH
& DECEMBER FLOWERS
club lingerie
sunday may 27th

The Mystery

I will wait until all is uncovered
I place all the pieces discovered
In hand
The question whose answer escapes
In time all the hurt will diminish
I grow from the painful resistance
And seek
The answer my question demands

The mystery keeps haunting me
Every clue is another it seems
High and low I will search
All my time it is worth
To learn what happiness means

To Hell with the pain I've been given
I must tie the hands of the villain, myself
The first step of the journey ahead
Through lies all the truth has been covered
Each day how the wall became tougher to climb
This I will never forget

The mystery keeps haunting me
Every clue is another it seems
High and low I will search
All my time it is worth
To learn what happiness means

I step with no safety net
Let my tears be no cry for help
Never again will you see
Hurt in my eyes

October Moon

Shattering of silence. Rumbles from an unopened cage
Cages there are some that should be unopened

It's part of an old song. A song for all to see
A song I sometimes forget. Now I remember it

Here is another love story
Here is another love story
Ending
October Moon
October moon again you've torn all from me

It starts so innocent. Subtle shakes, my eyes open
Jars my memory, tired habits die in me
Forever I don't know, today I recognized
Bare my tired expression
Forget me as I walk away

Here is another love story
Here is another love story
Ending
October moon
October moon again
You've torn all from me

Into my soul you reach
And steal my family, dignity
My giving love away

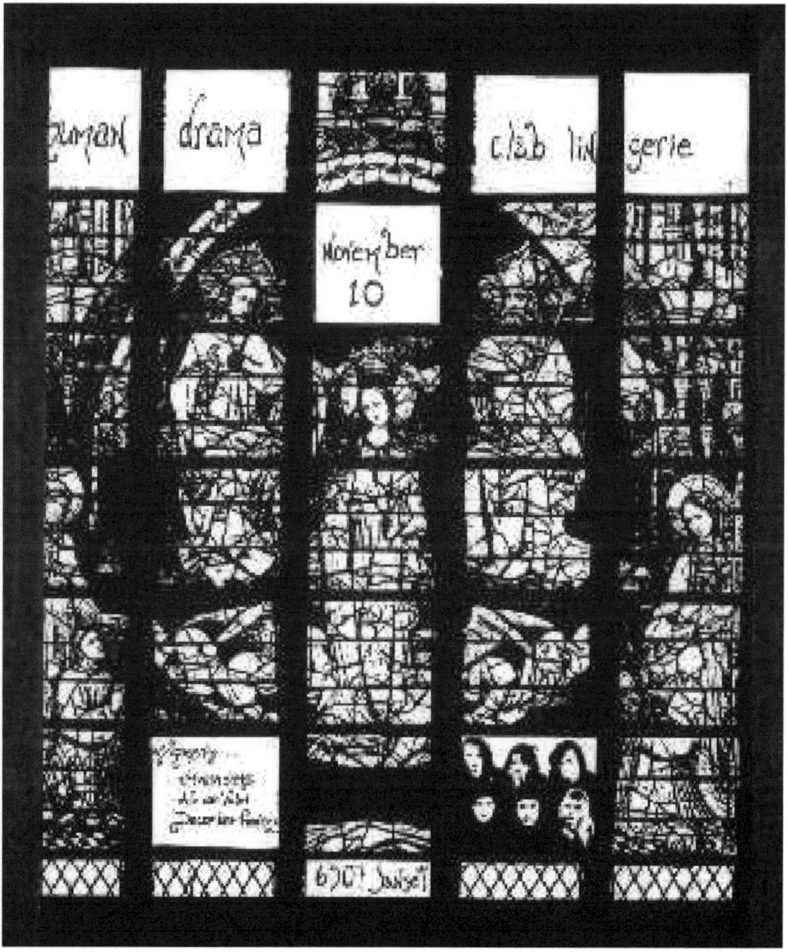

drama
november
10
lin gerie

The Art of Seduction

My mind is miles away. Half-hearted answers
Mind on the TV screen. Today's old news
But there's a tension I don't understand
And it's holding my hand
There's a pull that I've never felt before

The art of seduction I can't follow
I can't move a muscle
The art of seduction

Confusion closes my eyes. Attempted warnings
Surface as broken words from trembling lips
There's a feeling it's never going to end
Wondering how it ever began
Wishing it had never gone so far
When seduction has torn me apart

The art of seduction
I can't follow
I can't move a muscle
The art of seduction

Shot on sight feel left for dead
Will conquers strength when it isn't a game
I don't touch what I don't understand
I close my eyes and feel no pain. I feel no pain

The art of seduction
I can't follow
I can't move a muscle
The art of seduction

Sound of the Blue Heart:
"Moonlight Over My Tears"

Hear the sidewalk speak. It tells a different tale with every step
Pieces of my heart lie like children lost so hopelessly
Two names carved in stone, but our street I walk alone
The innocence of that day still in the air
A clock that tells no time
But following I feel the sentence of the crime

Silver light cuts through darkened skies
All trapped inside
Push from my eyes and shine moonlight over my tears

A river rushes by two lovers eye to eye not noticing
You can see their breath. The cold so easily they forget
To here the sidewalk leads
The place you laid your head where forever rose from its death
And the clock tells no time. Now weary from my climb
Following I feel the sentence for the crime

Silver light cuts through darkened skies
All trapped inside
Push from my eyes and shinemoonlight over my tears

...Our love, our hate, my trust, our lies, every step,every breath, every
beat of our heart, every way to say I love you, your hands, your touch,
your mouth, your words, the promises, the child, the family, the life,
our death...
..FOREVER

Hear the sidewalk speak. It tells a different tale with every step
Still the clock, it tells no time. The hands support my climb
But following I feel the sentence of the crime

Silver light cuts through darkened skies
All trapped inside
Push from my eyes and shine moonlight over my tears

Sound of the Blue Heart:
"Where Love Carries Me"

You beg for the earth and the sun and moon
I gave that and my soul to you
When you said there was a new way I should walk
I walked that line for you
You took until I had no more
Then claimed you sank from the weight of my world
Screamed you were a woman then said
"Don't you know I'm just a little girl"

Is there a picture I have not seen? The truth beneath the skin
I ask is the image you reveal only what you think I long to see
How can words like love and trust flow from your lips so easily
You say these words so well but run in fear from what they mean

There is a hole where you can hide. No escape is your excuse
A finger pointed to the blind. For your escape I have no use
Here is the question on my mind, Should I forgive so easily
The only answer I can find, I stand where love carries me

Your ways of torture spill into a river you cannot heal
And the river flows into my heart drowning hope, I fear
We were both trapped too long in the prison of your charm
Every time you said you found the key it just led us to another fall

There is a hole where you can hide. No escape is your excuse
A finger pointed to the blind. For your escape I have no use
Here is the question on my mind, should I forgive so easily
The only answer I can find, I stand where love carries me

If I could find a different way to feel, I'd feel that way for you
Or erase every second of you inside, Yeah that's what I'd do
But I know better then that, I wish it wasn't true
So I just settle for the mirror you must look into
There is a hole where you can hide...

lyrics by   S.J. Indovina Jr & Anne Kadrovich

Sound of the Blue Heart:
"Admission"

Gather round me all who do believe
Call together all who fantasize
That there is an end to all of this
Open your heart reveal the love
I say a prayer for what is left
That there is an end to all of this

We take the scar we understand
But keep it far beneath our skin
Swear this is the end. Then we do it again

You are what you are. Show what you believe
Mistakes are all around. Save only what needs to live
Eyes only see tears from battles past we fear
To victory we are blind. The loss we can't admit

Words polish all that will not shine
Fake shock at the ruins when revealed
Deny it all but it lies with you still
You can run but you cannot hide
You can never leave your thoughts behind
You can try but you never will

Save only what you feel needs to be saved
Only hold what has held you before
And bring an end
To all of this

You are what you are
Show what you believe
Mistakes are all around
Save only what needs to live
Eyes only see tears
From battles past we fear
To victory we are blind

The loss we can't admit

About Michelle

Shaken by complicated thoughts, yearning for simplicity
She works so hard, only to hide
Only to hide behind her camouflage
For the curious she has no time
She'd rather stay inside

Once I caught a glimpse of her
And through her crystal blue eyes saw
All the way to her heart
Through all barriers

There are no pearls in her life. Only cheap imitations
That she sometimes allows herself to see as real
For a moment or two there is a mothers love
Religion she never found
And the one who could replace her mother and god
Here on earth

Once I caught a glimpse of her
And through her crystal blue eyes saw
All the way to her heart
No barriers

I saw a sea of tears, a thousand unused smiles
I saw the hope that comes from dreams
Where we all know about Michelle

Michelle would you notice if the walls would fall?
Would you notice if I tried to chip away?
For lack of love do you hate?
Don't you know it's yourself you punish
Listen hard.
Do you wonder what this song is about?

Once I caught a glimpse of her
And through her crystal blue eyes saw
All the way to her heart
Through all barriers

Your Fire

For the first time in my life words escape me
I stand unarmed
How do I tell you the tears you shed are mine

For the first time in my life it isn't easy
All is right, all is wrong
I will love you anyway you want
Or all ways if you choose

There is room for your fire here
I can feel the way it burns
I want to be the one that you run to when you're scared

With every step your body trembles
With every touch I'm taken in
Met by the beauty and the pain of what your life is

There is room for your fire here
I can feel the way it burns
I want to be the one that you run to
When you're scared

For the first time in my life I have no fear
Of what another brings
I give to you knowing what you take I will never lose

There is room for your fire here
I can feel the way it burns
I want to be the one that you run to when you're scared

I Wish I Could See

On the avenue you walk across, swirling in and out without looking up
Are those your chains on the ground
Proclaiming freedom from our world, binding rules on the ground
Binding rules on the ground

I wish I could see through your eyes
I wish I could feel what's inside of you

I pray for your every chance. Unsettling mind, I'll be the last
Because followers always wait. The cushion can't break our fall
Breaking our arms on the binding rules
Breaking our arms

I wish I could see through your eyes
I wish I could feel what's inside of you

I curse the eyes that curse you from far away
The limited ones who live and die and never change
Raised by fathers before who scream and praise ,"He's just like me."
And gladly lend the chains. And gladly lend the chains

I wish I could see through your eyes
I wish I could feel what's inside of you

When I feel the way I do stripped to see through and through
What was true, it isn't true anymore
Right and wrong on the floor

I curse the eyes that curse you

I wish I could see through your eyes
I wish I could feel what's inside of you

Is It Love Or Hate

Father can you hear me? Can you see me round the bend
Or am I still a child sharing smiles with an imaginary friend
And I know you're disappointed with who I really am
So you lose yourself in lost little days
And laughter that won't come again
What I've been given you cannot take
I'm your favorite stranger and your perfect mistake

Is it love or hate?
Are we to the point of giving
For giving's sake
Is it love or hate?
We've come to the final hour
A choice we must make

Father who are you? It's a mystery to me
And it's a thankless job being what you want me to be
My future it gets so damn lost in all your history
What's the sense making you proud
If it leaves me so empty
But it isn't all your fault I fight who I am
And I beat myself black and blue
I can't lose for winning

Is it love or hate?
Are we to the point of giving
For giving's sake
Is it love or hate?
We've come to the final hour
A choice we must make

lyrics by S.J. Indovina Jr. & Greg Slugocki

Lost

Circled by shadow for so long
The fear of what is right or wrong
Resentment bred by giving oh the cost

I am here. I am not here
I am lost

Angered by the love the pain I cannot hide
The house I labored to build I cannot find
A touch so strong the strength that once was

Is it here? It is not here
It is lost

Flicker flame as I rest my head
Held in the clutches of regret
I go to trance in the candle red

With every breath and step the search goes on
With every day I discover I am torn
Did love lie beside me once?

And is it here. It is not here
It is lost

Am I here?
I am not here
I am lost

I am here
Here
Lost

Lonely

Ashes fall from the cigarette of the man who can't forget
Who learns more from a single second of silence
Than from any word ever spoken to him
Any poem misunderstood
Or from every second of his past that haunts him

Could I be more lonely?
I don't know...

Put in front of the mirror, why he can't recall
As he stares into the scars he cannot cover
But to all eyes laid upon him
But to all the hands that try to hold him
The pain still hides beneath the surface

Could I be more lonely?
I don't know if I could

Night passes behind him but he doesn't turn to look
The shackles and the gag will not allow it
"So far am I from caring," he says
"Or do I care too much"
For the more I give the more I must be given

Could I be more lonely?
I don't know if I could

I Am Not Here

I draw a parallel from days gone by
When glory laid in our arms
Simple pleasures now are not so simple
Once it was enough just to be near

From my eyes look away. (They can't see)
From my hands turn away. (I can't feel)
From my heart look away
I am not here

You stand torn my greatest treasure
looking for another chance to sleep
I promise I will be here when you wake up
Tell me what can you promise me

From my eyes look away. (They can't see)
From my hands turn away. (I can't feel)
From my heart look away
I am not here

You say it's me that you love completely
As you lie in your lovers arms
I can see your bruises oh so clearly
Can you see what he's done to me

From my eyes look away. (They can't see)
From my hands turn away. (I can't feel)
From my heart look away
I am not here

Goodnight Sweetheart

Sweetheart can you hear me
I'm a hundred million miles from you today
All we treasured, all we promised
Flew out the window of our heart
A love we'd never seen as strong
I guess baby life was just too much for us

All the tears I cried for you
All the hope I never knew
To think I'll never hold your hand
Touch your face
Or look into your eyes again
The way we looked in no other eyes before
And never will
Again

Darling it's not all right now
Don't misunderstand what I say
My greatest fear stands before me
If blood is life you are my blood
The reason I wake up
Only you lie next to me no more

All the tears I cried for you
All the hope I never knew
To think I'll never hold your hand
Touch your face
Or look into your eyes again
The way we looked in no other eyes before
And never will
Again

Why did we fall?
It is just the human curse we failed to beat
To our weakness we turned a blind eye
And our innocence led us into the trap
With flesh and bones we could not lift out
The heart we worked so hard to fill

The Truth About Gina

Gina tries to understand
Why she holds so little in her hands
And how she can't remember
What has passed through

A mirror finds wet Gina's eyes
For reasons unidentified
. And if you ask her why
She says "I never cry"

But far beyond
Her calm expression lies
The truth

An image of a little girl
Flashes now in an older world
Before she was taught to need
And learned to want

You can ask her but never understand
The pain as my innocence burns
She says "I was made a child,
That is what I am"

But far beyond
Her calm expression lies
The truth

The truth she denies
So not to face battered innocence
Little memories carry her away
with every beginning comes an ending
So to child she returns

Gina tries to understand
Why she holds so little in her hand
And how she can't remember
What has passed through

Look at Me Now

This is a different story
I've turned another page
My hands are weaker
And my eyes are showing age

I never wanted much from life, only what is real
Real is something the mind creates
And the heart believes

Don't promise me anything
I cannot believe
Because I once did
And look at me now

I followed you so far down. I still can't get out
I see my face in the mirror
But I don't recognize my thoughts

I lived on your lies for so long
I became cynical
I wrote twenty fucked up songs
About trust, love and hope

Don't promise me anything
I cannot believe
Because I once did
And look at me now

This is no love story
Just the opposite you see
It's about how the promise of it
Blinded me

A Song About Us

This is a song about life. This is a song about life
This is a song about life. And I'm so afraid

This is a song about trust. Believing made fools out of us
This is a song about trust. I'm so afraid

This is a song about truth
Sung from the wilderness in which we search
If this is a song about truth, I'm so afraid

This is a song about God. I am as much him as you are
If this is a song about God, I'm so afraid

If time heals all wounds
What heals the pain I feel from it passing
Time is all that leaves, I'm afraid

Beware what lies ahead?
What lies behind is what haunts me
So this is a song about tomorrow, And I'm afraid

This is a song about home, and it's taking too long to get there
This is a song about home, and I'm afraid

I'm afraid to call anything mine. Surely time will take it from me
Yet I'll remember how it felt. Of that I'm afraid

This is a song about hope. Come on all you fools sing along
This is the only song about hope, so sing along

This is a song about dreams
Wake up, pretend you don't know what they mean
Yeah this song is just a dream, but I'm so afraid

This is a song about me
And this is a song about you
I guess this is a song about us
I'm afraid

King of Loneliness

I am searching for the missing
Piece that makes me whole
The hate I feel for what I have become
Allows me no control
Truth has all but vanished from
All I say and do
If wishes did come true I'd wish
For the purity I once knew

I'm past the point of no return
I'm past the point of caring
I have screamed as loud
As I can scream
No one ever listens

I am king of loneliness
I can't give this crown away
From never wanting anything
I've got too much of nothing

As a boy I did believe
If I closed my eyes I would disappear
But I would always open them
For fear it would be true
Too much time spent inside
And childhood logic realized
Look I have disappeared
I closed my eyes too long

I'm past the point of no return

"I've never been able to be really open or relate very well one on one or in a social atmosphere. Here I trace it back to childhood and actual thoughts I had. Why did songwriting come so easy ? At the actual point of creation I am always alone."...JI

Acknowledgements:

Very special thanks to Megan Ducker for her time and energy completing this book. To Scott Ducker and Jimi Demmitt for their assistance. To Lance Davis for making this a reality. I am not worthy of such friends.

Thanks also to Dave Eddy, Anthony Zaragoza, Christian and Melissa Serpas, and my wonderful family; Dixie, Sam, and Dee.

I have been fortunate enough to play with some amazing players, all of whom I would like to thank: Michael Ciravolo, Charles Bouis, Mark Balderas, C.J. Eiriksson, Steve Caton, Rita D'Albert, Curt Harding, Carlo Bartolini, Jamii Szmadzinski, Geri Sutyak, Lynne Bertles, Michael Mallory, Chris Rezanson, Laura Laird, Dusty Jones, Lili Haydn, Renelle LaPlante, Chris Lizzotte, Estefan Bravo, Lisa Meuret, William Dolan, Lance Tamanaha, Jim Wirt, Steve Fuxan, Chuck Jonau, Chuck Jung, Chaz Waltz, Roger Sause, Phillip Stephenson, Roger Berg, Patric Mata, Jeff Russo, Dimitri Ioffe, Lisa Haney, Julia Kent, Clive Wright, Anne Kadrovich, Lisa Marie Lyou

Transcriptions by Megan Ducker
Design by Dave Eddy
Layout by Dave Eddy, Megan Ducker, Jimi Demmitt

Photos: Doug Churchill, Keena, Valerie, Ed Colver, Dave Eddy, Jeff Katz, Tracey Davenport, Amanda Spiva, Susan Jennings, Kathy Wallenbrock, Melinda Lewis

Visit Human Drama in cyberspace:
http://home.earthlink.net/~cinexl/hdhp.html
email: hdrama1@aol.com